T0199014

This is my book:

_____

AuthorHouse™
1663 Liberty Drive
Bloomington, IN 47403
www.authorhouse.com
Phone: 833-262-8899

Because of the dynamic nature of the Internet, any web addresses or links contained in this book may have changed
since publication and may no longer be valid. The views expressed in this work are solely those of the author and do
not necessarily reflect the views of the publisher, and the publisher hereby disclaims any responsibility for them.

Any people depicted in stock imagery provided by Getty Images are models,
and such images are being used for illustrative purposes only.
Certain stock imagery © Getty Images.

This book is printed on acid-free paper.

ISBN: 978-1-6655-7750-2 (sc)
ISBN: 978-1-6655-7751-9 (e)

Published by AuthorHouse 07/21/2023

My Mommy Is Having A Baby

by glendalee

This book is dedicated to:

Michael Paul,

Thank you for having the courage to come to me and share your true feelings and for loving your baby sister so much.

Seeing the world through your eyes has made me aware of so much. Thank you for showing me how.

You fill my heart with joy and overflowing love. Yes! You are worthy of love and worthy of all your dreams coming true.

I love you unconditionally, with all my heart, forever and ever.

Mom

Hi! I am Michael Paul.

I'd like to tell you a story about a time when my mommy
was having a baby and how that made me feel.

My mommy is having a baby!
I'm scared and upset.
Am I still worthy of my mommy's love?
Will Mommy have time for me?
She's my mommy; do I have to share her now?

I asked my friend how he felt when his
mommy was having a baby.
He said he felt the same way as I do.
His mommy did not have time for him because babies
can't do anything for themselves and take a lot of time.
My mommy's having a baby!

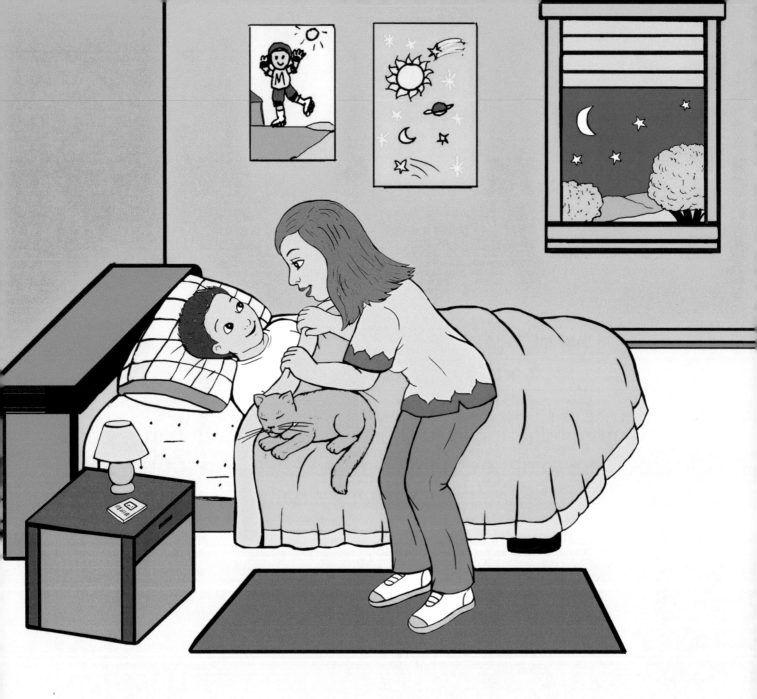

My best friend knew his mommy loved him because she
sat next to him and read him a storybook every night.
Then she pulled the blankets up when he was in his bed.
My mommy's having a baby!

I asked my mommy to sit next to me and read me a storybook every night and pull my blankets up when I am in my bed.

And Mommy said, "Yes, I will!"

My mommy's having a baby!

When Mommy spends time with me too,
I feel special and worthy of love.

I *am* loved.

Because I feel loved, it is easy for me to love
our new baby and laugh and smile.

My mommy had a baby!

My friend and I are very thankful and
no longer scared or upset.

We are full of love and joy.

My mommy had a baby!

Now I can be happy because I know Mommy
has time for me and the baby–just like I have
time for Mommy and my best friend!
Everything is possible when you know you are loved.

We have a baby!